THE FASTEST
DINOSAURS

BY "DINO" DON LESSEM
ILLUSTRATIONS BY JOHN BINDON

LERNER PUBLICATIONS COMPANY / MINNEAPOLIS

To Peter Lessem, my favorite brother

Text copyright © 2005 by Dino Don, Inc.
Illustrations copyright © 2005 by John Bindon
The photographs in this book appear courtesy of: American Museum of Natural History, p. 12; Animals, Animals © OSF/BARTLETT, D&J, p. 13; Royal Tyrrell Museum of Palaeontology, p. 14; © Pat Crowe, p. 31.

This book is available in two editions:
Library binding by Lerner Publications Company,
    a division of Lerner Publishing Group
Soft cover by First Avenue Editions,
    an imprint of Lerner Publishing Group
241 First Avenue North
Minneapolis, MN 55401 U.S.A.

Website address: www.lernerbooks.com

Library of Congress Cataloging-in-Publication-Data

Lessem, Don.
    The fastest dinosaurs / by Don Lessem ; illustrations by John Bindon.
       p.   cm. — (Meet the dinosaurs)
    Includes index.
    ISBN: 0-8225-1422-2 (lib. bdg. : alk. paper)
    ISBN: 0-8225-2620-4 (pbk. : alk. paper)
    1. Dinosaurs—Juvenile literature. 2. Animal locomotion—Juvenile literature. I. Bindon, John. II. Title.
QE861.5.L476 2005
567.9—dc22   2004007055

Manufactured in the United States of America
1 2 3 4 5 6 – DP – 10 09 08 07 06 05

TABLE OF CONTENTS

MEET THE
FASTEST DINOSAURS

WELCOME, DINOSAUR FANS!

I'm "Dino" Don. I love all dinosaurs. Everyone knows about giant dinosaurs like *Brachiosaurus*. They ran about as fast as the plants they ate. But some dinosaurs were very fast runners. Have you heard of these speedy dinosaurs? You'll find out about them here. Have fun!

GALLIMIMUS (GAL-ih-MY-muhs)
Length: 17 feet
Home: central Asia
Time: 70 million years ago

GASPARINISAURA (gas-pahr-EE-nee-SAWR-uh)
Length: 2.5 feet
Home: South America
Time: 84 million years ago

MICRORAPTOR (MY-kroh-RAP-tohr)
Length: 1.8 feet
Home: Asia
Time: 124 million years ago

ORNITHOMIMUS (ohr-NITH-oh-MY-muhs)
Length: 12 feet
Home; western North America
Time: 65 million years ago

STRUTHIOMIMUS (STROOTH-ee-oh-MY-muhs)
Length: 13 feet
Home: western North America
Time: 76 million years ago

TROODON (TROH-uh-dahn)
Length: 6 feet
Home: western North America
Time: 76 million years ago

VELOCIRAPTOR (veh-LAHS-ih-RAP-tohr)
Length: 6.5 feet
Home: central Asia
Time: 80 million years ago

THE RACE IS ON

A huge *Tarbosaurus* is closing in. The
long-legged *Gallimimus* doesn't see the
predator coming. *Tarbosaurus* reaches
out to bite. At last, *Gallimimus* spots the
hunting dinosaur and turns to run.

Tarbosaurus lunges. But the smaller dinosaur's long legs move quickly. *Gallimimus* darts away. It moves much more quickly than *Tarbosaurus*. In a moment, it is safe again.

THE TIME OF THE FASTEST DINOSAURS

Microraptor

Velociraptor

124 million
years ago

80 million
years ago

Dinosaurs first appeared nearly 230 million years ago. Back then, giant reptiles were the earth's fiercest animals. These animals had scaly skin. Some dinosaurs did too. But dinosaurs weren't reptiles. Dinosaurs walked on straight legs. Most reptiles have bent legs.

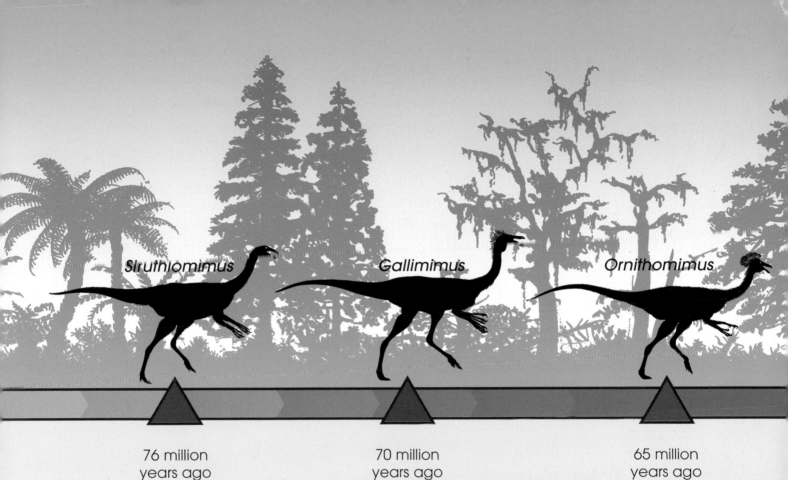

Struthiomimus

Gallimimus

Ornithomimus

76 million
years ago

70 million
years ago

65 million
years ago

Straight legs helped some dinosaurs run
faster than reptiles. Speed may have
helped dinosaurs survive and grow in
numbers. Over time, many giant reptiles
died out. Dinosaurs then ruled the earth for
more than 160 million years.

DINOSAUR FOSSIL FINDS

The numbers on the map on page 11 show some of the places where people have found fossils of the dinosaurs in this book. You can match each number on the map to the name and picture of the dinosaurs on this page.

1. Gallimimus   2. Gasparinisaura   3. Microraptor   4. Ornithomimus

5. Struthiomimus   6. Troodon   7. Velociraptor

Dinosaurs lived all over the world. Their **fossils** have been found in many places. Fossils are traces left behind by something that lived long ago. Bones, teeth, and skin fossils help scientists think about how dinosaurs might have looked.

Fossils also show clues about how dinosaurs cared for their babies. Fossils helped us learn how some dinosaurs moved from place to place in groups. And by studying fossils, we've figured out how fast dinosaurs could run.

Fossils of footprints tell us the most about dinosaur speed. Scientists measure the distance between the footprints. This distance is called the **stride length.** A long stride length means long, fast legs.

Next, scientists compare the dinosaur to a living animal. For instance, an ostrich is about the same size and shape as some dinosaurs. Scientists measure and ask questions. How fast does the ostrich run? What is its stride length? The answers help us figure out how fast some dinosaurs ran.

Bone fossils tell us about speed too. Meat-eating dinosaurs had hollow bones. A hollow bone is filled with air. It weighs less than bones that aren't hollow. The fastest dinosaurs, like this *Ornithomimus,* had light bodies and long, hollow leg bones.

Some dinosaurs were very heavy, like this
Gastonia. With thick leg bones and plates
of armor, these dinosaurs couldn't run fast.
Perhaps they couldn't run at all. But their
armor protected them from attack.

REASONS TO RUN

A young *Abelisaurus* on the hunt spots a little plant eater called *Gasparinisaura*. She's taking care of her babies in her nest. She can't run away without leaving the nest. Will *Abelisaurus* attack her?

Another *Gasparinisaura* darts in front of
the killer dinosaur. The hunter chases him
instead. But *Gasparinisaura* is too quick.
Soon the tired *Abelisaurus* gives up the hunt.

Troodon was the smartest of all dinosaurs. It was fast too. This *Troodon* has spotted a small, ratlike animal. The animal is too quick for most dinosaurs to catch.

The animal runs toward its hole. It zigzags in different directions to escape. But *Troodon* can twist and turn just as quickly. It closes in on the animal and grabs it for a tasty dinner.

A pack of *Velociraptor* dinosaurs is hunting a young *Pinacosaurus*. The **prey** is only the size of a sheep. The hunters are even smaller. They're no bigger than a fourth grader. But they work together and run fast.

Speed was very helpful to meat-eating
dinosaurs. They had to be faster than their
prey to catch a meal. But *Velociraptor* had
more than speed. Its sharp claws and team
attack made it very deadly.

THE FASTEST OF ALL

In Asia's Gobi Desert, *Gallimimus* are on the run from a sandstorm. These strange dinosaurs have thin claws and no teeth. They look like fast-running birds called ostriches. In fact, *Gallimimus* and their relatives are known as ostrich dinosaurs.

The ostrich dinosaurs are the fastest of all
dinosaurs. *Gallimimus* are so fast that they
will outrun the sandstorm and get to safety.
Many slower dinosaurs will not escape.

Ornithomimus roamed western North America 65 million years ago. Like modern birds, *Ornithomimus* had no teeth and hollow bones. This dinosaur's hollow bones helped make it speedy.

Scientists think that *Ornithomimus* chased
down tiny creatures, such as lizards,
mammals, and insects. It snapped up these
meals with its toothless beak. This baby
Ornithomimus is about to catch a moth.

A flooding river is washing over the land.
Animals are running for their lives. One
of them is most likely to make it to high
ground. It is *Struthiomimus.* This fast ostrich
dinosaur is as long as a classroom.

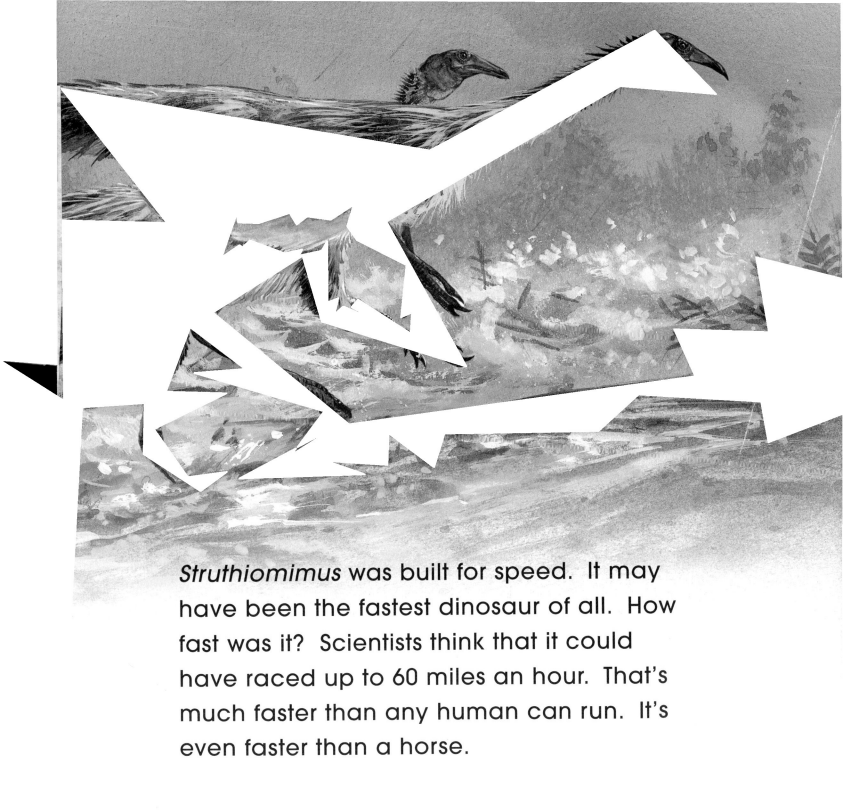

Struthiomimus was built for speed. It may have been the fastest dinosaur of all. How fast was it? Scientists think that it could have raced up to 60 miles an hour. That's much faster than any human can run. It's even faster than a horse.

THE END?

Many scientists think that a huge rock from space hit the earth about 65 million years ago. The crash would have raised clouds of dust and smoke. Dinosaurs could have run away from the clouds. But even the fastest could not have escaped.

That's because the clouds would have changed the earth's weather. Many scientists think that those changes wiped out all the dinosaurs.

Long before this time, many fast dinosaurs traveled the earth. Some had feathers. These tiny *Microraptor* do. Feathers helped keep small dinosaurs warm. But some scientists think that feathers helped some dinosaurs move around.

Microraptor's feathers and speed might
have helped it take off into the air. If that is
true, the fastest dinosaurs may not be gone
for good. Over time, they may have
become the animals we know as birds!

GLOSSARY

fossils (FAH-suhlz): the remains, tracks, or traces of something that lived long ago

mammals (MAM-uhlz): animals that feed their babies milk and have hair on their bodies

predator (PREH-duh-tur): an animal that hunts and eats other animals

prey (PRAY): an animal that other animals hunt and eat

stride length (STRYD LENKTH): the distance between an animal's footprints

INDEX